SandCastle™
Animal Groups

A School of Fish

ANIMAL GROUPS
IN THE OCEAN

Alex Kuskowski

CONSULTING EDITOR, DIANE CRAIG, M.A./READING SPECIALIST

A Division of ABDO
ABDO
Publishing Company

visit us at www.abdopublishing.com

Published by ABDO Publishing Company, a division of ABDO, P.O. Box 398166, Minneapolis, Minnesota 55439. Copyright © 2013 by Abdo Consulting Group, Inc. International copyrights reserved in all countries. No part of this book may be reproduced in any form without written permission from the publisher. SandCastle™ is a trademark and logo of ABDO Publishing Company.

Printed in the United States of America, North Mankato, Minnesota
062012
092012

 PRINTED ON RECYCLED PAPER

Editor: Liz Salzmann
Content Developer: Nancy Tuminelly
Cover and Interior Design and Production: Anders Hanson, Mighty Media, Inc.
Photo Credits: Shutterstock

Library of Congress Cataloging-in-Publication Data
Kuskowski, Alex.
  A school of fish : animal groups in the ocean / Alex Kuskowski.
    p. cm. -- (Animal groups)
  ISBN 978-1-61783-541-4
  1. Marine animals--Behavior--Juvenile literature. 2. Social behavior in animals--Juvenile literature. I. Title.
  QL122.2.K87 2013
  591.77--dc23
                         2012009032

SANDCASTLE™ LEVEL: FLUENT

SandCastle™ books are created by a team of professional educators, reading specialists, and content developers around five essential components—phonemic awareness, phonics, vocabulary, text comprehension, and fluency—to assist young readers as they develop reading skills and strategies and increase their general knowledge. All books are written, reviewed, and leveled for guided reading, early reading intervention, and Accelerated Reader® programs for use in shared, guided, and independent reading and writing activities to support a balanced approach to literacy instruction. The SandCastle™ series has four levels that correspond to early literacy development. The levels are provided to help teachers and parents select appropriate books for young readers.

Emerging Readers
(no flags)

Beginning Readers
(1 flag)

Transitional Readers
(2 flags)

Fluent Readers
(3 flags)

Contents

Animals in the Ocean | 4

Why Live in a Group? | 6

A Bloom of Jellyfish | 8

A Cast of Crabs | 10

A Shiver of Sharks | 12

A Waddle of Penguins | 14

A Team of Dolphins | 16

A School of Fish | 18

A Colony of Sea Lions | 20

More Ocean Groups | 22

Quiz | 23

Glossary | 24

Animals in the Ocean

Oceans are huge bodies of water. Many animals live in the ocean. Some animals come to the **surface** to breathe air. Other animals can breathe underwater.

Why Live in a Group?

Animals often live in groups. Animals in a group can **protect** each other. They can share space, food, and water. They also work together to help raise babies. Many animal groups have fun names!

A Bloom of Jellyfish

Jellyfish gather in blooms. They are pushed together by ocean **currents**. Sometimes thousands of jellyfish end up in the same place!

Jellyfish Names

MALE
boar

BABY
ephyra

FEMALE
sow

GROUP
bloom, smack

A Cast of Crabs

A group of crabs is called a cast. Crabs **communicate** by waving their **pincers**.

Crab Names

MALE
cock

BABY
larvae, zoea, megalops

FEMALE
hen

GROUP
cast, consortium

A Shiver of Sharks

Hammerhead sharks swim in a shiver. They are the only sharks that swim in a group. They hunt fish during the day.

Shark Names

MALE
male, bull

BABY
cub, pup

FEMALE
female

GROUP
shiver, frenzy

A Waddle of Penguins

A group of emperor penguins is called a waddle. Emperor penguins spend half their lives in the ocean. When they hunt, they can dive 1,800 feet (550 m) deep!

Penguin Names

MALE
male

BABY
chick, nestling

FEMALE
female

GROUP
waddle, rookery

A Team of Dolphins

Dolphins are very smart. A team of dolphins works together to catch fish. First they herd the fish into a group. Then the dolphins take turns eating the fish.

Dolphin Names

MALE
bull

FEMALE
cow

BABY
calf, pup

GROUP
team, school, pod, herd

A School of Fish

Fish swim together in schools. Fish in schools watch one another to find food. When one fish finds food, the other fish begin to look for food too.

Fish Names

MALE
male

FEMALE
female

BABY
fry, fingerling

GROUP
school, shoal

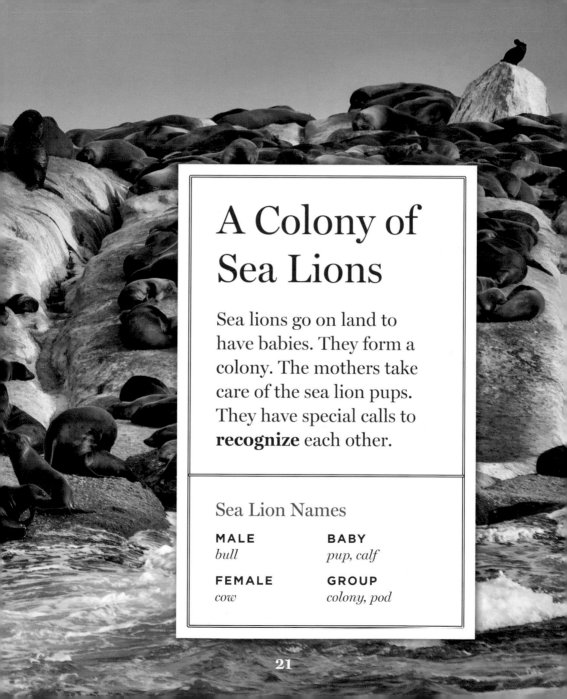

A Colony of Sea Lions

Sea lions go on land to have babies. They form a colony. The mothers take care of the sea lion pups. They have special calls to **recognize** each other.

Sea Lion Names

MALE
bull

BABY
pup, calf

FEMALE
cow

GROUP
colony, pod

More

OCEAN GROUPS

A troop of
dogfish

A swarm
of eel

A risk of
lobster

A bed of
oysters

A gam of
whales

A pod of
porpoises

A herd of
walruses

Quiz

1. Oceans are very small bodies of water. *True or false?*

2. Crabs **communicate** by waving their **pincers**. *True or false?*

3. Hammerhead sharks hunt for fish. *True or false?*

4. An emperor penguin spends its whole life in the ocean. *True or false?*

5. In a school, if one fish finds food, the other fish do nothing. *True or false?*

Glossary

communicate – to share ideas, information, or feelings.

current – a steady flow of movement in a liquid or a gas.

pincer – the claw of an animal such as a crab or scorpion.

protect – to guard someone or something from harm or danger.

recognize – to know and remember.

surface – the top of a body of water.